PUSHKIN PRESS

THE BOY WHO STOLE ATTILA'S HORSE

An *Irish Times* Book of the Year

'A deeply unsettling but compelling novella with all the visceral, elemental force of myth and folktale'

The Lady

'Big-picture writing at its most imaginative and unpredictable'

Huffington Post, 'Top Ten Political Books to Read in 2016'

'[A]bitter-sweet fable of our times… both tragic and a call to arms'

TLS

'[Its] language supports the story's imaginative breadth… witty and refreshing'

New Statesman

'Its depiction of madness is as affecting as any I've read in modern fiction… Seek out this treasure; prepare for a knock-out'

Big Issue

'Has the unfailing grimness of a fairytale… A dark allegory for modern capitalist society… explores the limits of the human mind and our enduring capacity for hope'

Booktrust

'Beyond brilliance… may well in time emerge as one of the most widely celebra

Eileen Batter

IVÁN REPILA (b. Bilbao, 1978) is a Spanish writer celebrated for the originality and depth of his prose. He worked in cultural management and as an editor, before turning to writing with his highly acclaimed debut novel, *Despicable Comedy*. *The Boy Who Stole Attila's Horse*, his second novel, is his first book to appear in English.

SOPHIE HUGHES is a literary translator and was previously an editor-at-large for *Asymptote Journal*. Her writing and translations have appeared in numerous publications, including the *Times Literary Supplement* and the *White Review*. She has also translated Rodrigo Hasbún's *Affections* for Pushkin Press.

Iván Repila

The Boy
Who Stole
Attila's
Horse

Translated by Sophie Hughes

PUSHKIN PRESS
LONDON

Pushkin Press
71–75 Shelton Street, London wc2h 9jq

Original text © 2013 Iván Repila

Published by arrangement with The Ella Sher Literary Agency

English translation © 2015 Sophie Hughes

Originally published in Spanish as
El niño que robó el caballo de Atila

This translation first published by Pushkin Press in 2015
This edition first published by Pushkin Press in 2016

1 3 5 7 9 8 6 4 2

ISBN 978 1 782272 22 9

Set in Monotype Baskerville by Tetragon, London
Printed by CPI Group (UK) Ltd, Croydon, CR0 4YY

www.pushkinpress.com

In a system of free trade and free markets poor countries—and poor people—are not poor because others are rich. Indeed, if others became less rich the poor would in all probability become still poorer.

MARGARET THATCHER

> I came to the cities in a time of disorder
> When hunger ruled.
> I came among men in a time of uprising
> And I revolted with them.
> So the time passed away
> Which on earth was given me.

BERTOLT BRECHT

'I T LOOKS IMPOSSIBLE to get out,' he says. And also: 'But we'll get out.'

To the north, the forest borders a mountain range and is surrounded by lakes so big they look like oceans. In the centre of the forest is a well. The well is roughly seven metres deep and its uneven walls are a bank of damp earth and roots, which tapers at the mouth and widens at the base, like an empty pyramid with no tip. The basin gurgles dark water, which filters along faraway veins and even more distant galleries that flow towards the river. It leaves a permanent muddy peat and sludge specked with bubbles that pop, spraying bursts of euca-lyptus back into the air. Whether due to pressure from the continental plates or the constant eddying breeze, the little roots move and turn and steer in a slow, sad dance, which evokes the nature of all the forests slowly absorbing the earth.

The older brother is big. With his hands he digs up lumps of sand to form a step strong enough to hold him, but when he lifts himself up in the air the weight of his body defeats him and the wall breaks.

The younger brother is small. He sits on the floor with his arms around his legs, blowing on a fresh graze on his knee. While thinking that the first blood always falls on the side of the weak, he watches his brother fall once, twice, three times.

'It hurts. I think it's broken.'

'Don't worry about the blood.'

Outside, the sun continues its loop and is eclipsed behind the mountains, drawing an afternoon shadow like a curtain over the well until it's barely possible to make out the pale cheeks, the eyeballs, the teeth. Attempts to carve a way out through the wall of earth have proved futile, and now Big is on his feet with his fingers hooked into the belt loops of his trousers, focused, searching the day's end for the answer to an enigma which fades as darkness falls.

'Up you get. You might be able to reach the edge if I put you on top of me.'

Small shudders, but he isn't cold.

'It's really high. We won't reach it,' he says, standing up.

Big takes Small by the hand and in one move lifts him up to his shoulders, as if they were playing at grown-ups and being as tall as a man. They steady themselves against the wall and from this position Small realizes that they won't be making it to any ledge.

'I don't reach. It's really high.'

Big grabs Small's feet firmly so he can lift him and increase their height by the entire length of his arms.

'What about now? Now do you reach?'

'No. Still no.'

'Are your arms stretched?'

'Of course!'

'Hold on then,' he says, and Big propels himself upwards and jumps as high as gravity and his legs allow him, emitting first a puff and then a kind of animal pant, full of rage, which his throat finally turns into a cry for help when they fall to the ground, hitting their elbows and backs against the soft mulch at the bottom.

'Was it close?'

'I don't know. I had my eyes shut,' Small says.

At night, the rustle of the forest is accompanied by a nagging buzz, the din of invisible jaws that inhabit the space like an amorphous mass. The brothers hug one another stretched out on the driest side of their new country, on a pelt of thick roots that enfolds them unresistingly. Neither of them sleeps, how could they?

At sunrise the well is a different colour. The dry earth on the higher part is composed of copper sediments, brownish-grey scars and yellow pine needles. Further down inside the well the earth is damp, black and blue, and the tips of the roots have a purplish glint. The sun is warm, and only the birds respond to the silence. Small's intestines gurgle under his hands.

'I'm hungry.'

Big rouses himself and tries to focus his vision with the turn of his neck. His sleep-stiffened muscles stretch from the Achilles tendon to the annulus of Zinn.

'We'll eat once we find a way out. Don't worry.'

'But I'm really hungry. My stomach hurts.'

'There's nothing to eat.'

'What do you mean there's nothing to eat? We've got the bag.'

Big remains silent for a second or two. The bag is in the corner of the well, rolled up in a muddy ball. Neither has touched it since they got there.

'The food in the bag is for Mother,' he says firmly.

Small pulls a face somewhere between resentment and resignation and gets up, supporting himself first with his hands on the floor, then on the wall. His brother lets out a pained sigh.

'We're getting out of here right now.'

They stretch out their limbs for a while, study the position of the sun to work out the time, and shout, calling for help. Afterwards, they grope the walls. They search them, scratch them, probe them for jutting fragments of rock, hardened snags, holes. They go on shouting. They repeat a few of their moves from yesterday afternoon, but barely raise themselves a couple of metres before they plummet back down to the bottom of the well. They dig up the earth looking for objects they might be able to use as a bridge: a large root, the remains of a trunk, anything. With each hour that passes they shout less. When the sun declares noon, pointing at the boys with his marble fingers, Big makes a decision.

'Hold on to my hands firmly. I'm going to throw you out of the well.'

Small suffers a fit of panic. The prospect of being thrown out of the well, as if he were a stone or a gun or any old object, makes him feel extraordinarily small, but his brother's resolve prevents him from protesting. After a few seconds of to and fro they manage to adopt the position required for the move; with their hands gripping on to the other's forearms they take slow breaths to quell the riot in their hearts, unsettled by the mystery of the exertion to come.

'I'm going to start spinning now. Don't be afraid. When you feel your legs lifting off the ground, let yourself be carried. We'll spin a little bit more to pick up speed and then I'll call out loud for you to let go of me. Have you got it?'

Small looks at his brother, amazed, as if seeing him for the first time. The image of his shattered body crosses his mind for an instant, leaving the taste of coins in his saliva.

'Are you sure?'

'I'm strong and you're small. I think I should give it a try.'

Then they take their positions: Big spreading his legs to steady himself when the speed picks up, Small with one knee on the ground so that he isn't dragged along, both of them gripping with such force that their knuckles blanch. And without another thought they start to spin. Big pulls his brother upwards so the rotation is clean and goes on spinning, and Small is raised a hand from the ground and he spins, another hand and he spins, until with the next spin he's virtually horizontal, with his eyes closed and his clenched teeth making dents in his gums; and still they spin, faster and faster, with each spin mapping a bigger circumference, and when it seems like they are at the point of falling, exhausted and breathless from so much spinning, Small slips down to the ground, but doesn't touch it, then soars back up at an angle, and they repeat this twice more, and in the final ascent Big shouts Now, and lets go, and with his eyes still closed Small breaks free and he takes off from the earth towards the sun like a comet of bones, and for just a few seconds he is flying, but he smashes, literally smashes into the wall, producing a dull crunch that drowns out any cry; and then, unconscious and bleeding from the mouth, he falls the few metres that separate him and the floor and lands on the dizzy body of his brother, like a circus act that ends in a bundle of piled up flesh, and no applause.

When he recovers, Big rinses the blood off his brother and cheerfully announces that apart from a few broken teeth and some bruises, it's nothing serious. Small protests:

'My whole body hurts. That didn't work. And I'm hungry.'

Big feels responsible for Small's injuries. He looks at him pityingly and ashamed, and then looks up at the spot against which he'd smashed him only seconds before. He gets up. Looking closer he sees the marks from the impact, the dent in the wall of earth. The cast has held the shape of the top half of his brother: the head, the torso, the arms. The missing teeth that they couldn't locate are probably still biting into the hollow. A smile spreads across Big's face. And though he knows he has had to use every ounce of his strength for that throw, a dark something awakens in him, a kind of mechanical resourcefulness that connects sequential layers of thought; a conspiracy of scattered images comes together and gives form to a pattern that is painful, but real. Afterwards, glowing with excitement, he goes back to Small. It's been twenty-four hours since they fell.

'I've had an idea,' he says. And also: 'But you have to make me a promise.'

2

I N THE BAG there is a loaf of bread.

When they go for food supplies, the brothers must take the dirt path that runs alongside their house up to the slope of bergamot trees, then rock-hop across the river and carry on beyond the wild cornfields. If they want to gain time, they must go through the forest. To do this means almost half a day's walk; double that if you count the return journey.

'I'm thirsty,' says Small.

'You can drink the water there on that side. I've already tried it. It's fresh.'

'But it's dirty.'

In the bag there is a loaf of bread and some dried tomatoes. Big goes towards the corner where the water flows more heavily, kneels down and digs a small hole. After a while the water builds up in the hole until it spills over. Big then sinks his head in the little well and drinks loudly, imitating a thirsty dog.

'It's good. Try it.'

Small copies all of his brother's gestures, including the nasty slurping sound.

'It tastes like dirt.'

'Everything here tastes like dirt. Get used to it.'

With his eyes on the bag, Small adds:

'Now I'm hungrier.'

Big takes the bag, twists it, and throws it to the opposite side of the well floor.

'I've told you already that we're not going to touch Mother's food. We'll eat what we have here.'

'But we don't have anything here.'

'Yes we do. You'll see.'

In the bag there is a loaf of bread, some dried tomatoes and a few figs. Big inspects every millimetre of the well, every cranny, every root. He makes a fold in his shirt and in the hollow collects everything he can find. Small watches him blankly. Afterwards, with black nails, Big sits down in front of his brother and unveils his booty of squashed ants, green snails, little yellow maggots, mushy roots and larvae.

'This is what we're going to eat.'

Small can't hide his disgust. He knows his brother is not joking, and that if he has made up his mind that they're going to eat grubs and weeds, grubs and weeds he will eat. He bites his lip to hold in the rising nausea and says:

'Fine.'

And he takes a handful of ants in his hand and tosses them into his mouth, swallowing them without chewing, almost without breathing. With his tongue he checks that there are none left between his teeth.

'Maybe if we added a little piece of tomato they'd be tastier,' he says with a weak smile.

In the bag there is a loaf of bread, some dried tomatoes, a few figs and a wedge of cheese. On hearing his brother's suggestion Big upends his shirt, scattering the food everywhere, and smacks him across the cheek with the back of his hand. His hand being so big, however, and the cheek so small, the blow also reaches Small's temple, his chin, and his ear. It connects, too, with his mouth and yanks the nerves in his teeth, pealing through the bone and making his gums flare. He falls flat on his back with half a lazy face, the flesh swelling with a pain so sharp it clouds his vision. And with his good ear he can still hear a voice bouncing between the walls, a deep echo that warns him:

'The bag isn't the solution. If you mention it again, I'll hold your head in the dirt until I kill you.'

In the bag there is a loaf of bread, some dried tomatoes, a few figs and a wedge of cheese.

Small never again repeats the word beginning with bee.

3

BY THE THIRD DAY they have developed a routine. When the sun comes up they drink water and gargle, then spit it out on the other side of the well in the same hole that they have dug for their waste deposits. Afterwards they take turns to shout, calling for help for several minutes at a time until their throats burn from the strain. For the rest of the morning Small busies himself collecting all manner of insects and roots, which he mashes in his shirt until they form a thick paste. Meanwhile, his brother does his exercises. Big builds up his muscles, adhering to a fixed regime, with push-ups to exercise his arms and shoulders, sets of sit-ups and then squats, which he does until his legs no longer obey him and he has to stop. He moves on to resistance training, lunging at different angles, strengthening his back and spine. To finish he repeats the push-ups, the sit-ups and the squats, but with his brother in tow so the session ends with him lifting Small up onto his shoulders, as if he were a weight bar or a sandbag. He rests for fifteen minutes and in this intermission the two brothers go back to their shouting, only stopping when they can no longer utter a word. Afterwards, Big repeats all of the exercises.

If they are able to look up at the sky without the sun burning their eyes they agree that the morning is over, and with that the afternoon begins. The distribution of food is totally unequal. Big eats eighty per cent of what his brother collects, leaving Small with what little he can extract from a worm, a few insects and two or three roots. Both sate their appetite in silence, and keep aside a small portion for supper. Once they have finished, they drink all the water they can and repeat their chorus of shouts. Afterwards, Small tucks himself into the foetal position, barely moving, and Big spends a couple of hours doing stretches. With the last light of the day they eat the vestiges of food that they left aside, still observing the same rationing model, and then go back to shouting until nightfall. They lie down pressed together, each of them searching in the other's body for some warmth to help him sleep. Meanwhile, the forest answers their daytime shouts with a nocturnal song. They await it restlessly, wondering whose they'll hear first: the crickets', the owls', or the wolves'.

5

S MALL DREAMS about a swarm of butterflies and watches himself catch them with his long, retractable tongue. If they are white, they taste of bread; if they are pink or red, of fruit—a combination of strawberries and oranges; the green ones taste of mint and peppermint; if they are dark they don't have a flavour—eating them is like licking windows.

The night before, a glow-worm fell into the well, which his brother devoured without batting an eyelid. In the dream, too, there are glow-worms, but they're big and you can't eat them, so he picks one and mounts her like an iridescent cavalryman. He is so hungry that he rides the glow-worm to a clearing set apart from the plain and when she stoops to let him down, he sinks his teeth into her side, tearing off pieces of luminous flesh, and drives his nails into her green haunch until he is in up to his hands, his elbows, the full length of his arms, and he slurps the glistening blood as if he were drinking raw egg out of the small crack in its shell. Satiated, and still atop the glowing body of his mount, he begins to cry, kicking himself, since without her, and in the terrible darkness that now covers him, he has no way of escaping the well.

In his dream the well is big like a city. Some say the citizens are all starving because the land exhausted itself. Small can't recall life outside of the well, but Big is older than him and remembers.

'They needed space up there,' he answers whenever Small asks why they live in such a rotten place.

'Are there many of them up there?'

'No, very few of them.'

'So above is small?'

'No. It's very big.'

'I don't understand.'

'Up there is where they hold the power.'

'What's that, then?'

A flying dog licks his horns, tickling him. His brother always talks like this, with few words, because he works a lot. For years he has been constructing a ladder out of liquorice laces in order to reach the edge of the well.

'Can I have a little nibble?'

'You know you can't. We need all of the laces.'

'I'm hungry.'

'So am I. But you ought to think about everyone, not just yourself.'

Small looks about him: there are people sleeping on the streets, children playing with talking flowers, men carrying babies in their marsupial pouches. There are others, like his brother, building contraptions in an attempt to get out of the well: a slate boat, a tower of clouds, a catapult made from the bones of the last dragon.

'I'm tired of thinking about everyone!'

Big lays another lace and a worm the shape of a chicken slips out from a hole. He wipes the sweat from his brow with his forearm and says:

'Once we are up there, we'll throw a party.'

'A party?'

'Yes.'

'The kind with balloons and lights and cakes?'

'No. The kind with rocks, torches and gallows.'

And, on dreaming of fire, suddenly he wakes up. He feels as if a flame has set alight the base of his skull or somewhere behind his eyes. The sky is only just beginning to let the light in and Big is sleeping, so Small gets up slowly, taking care not to wake him. With the taste of fluorescence still in his mouth he rummages among the roots for an ant or a worm. He knows that he is meant to follow the diet that his brother has devised for him strictly, but the hunger he feels on waking is hard to control. According to Big, he can go many days drinking the muddy water from the well, eating a few bugs and sucking on the tips of the roots. However, he stresses, he must remain as still as possible so as not to expend energy outside his hours of collecting.

He spots a small worm a metre away and moves closer, but just as he is about to trap it his stomach lets out a rising growl, which ricochets across the tapestry of earth hanging all around him. Something inside him jolts his guts with the lash of a whip. It's so loud that it seems like a ghostly echo from the well itself, and Big wakes up, sullen, orienting himself more with his ears than his eyes.

'What are you doing?'

'Nothing.'

'You're awake already? What was that noise?'

'Me.'

Big rubs his face and sees his brother fixed to the wall as if he formed part of it, stooped in the shape of a question mark.

'You made that noise? It sounded like mooing.'

'I think I'm breaking inside,' says Small.

The day passes without incident, continuing its round of fears and hopes. Nobody responds to their shouts but they are getting used to that. When night falls, Small clutches on to his brother tightly.

'I'm not feeling good.'

'I know. I can see it in your face. You've lost weight and you're weak.'

'Maybe I should eat more.'

'Not yet. Relax, you'll get used to the hunger. Your stomach is getting smaller each day, which is why it hurts: it's shrinking. Once it has shrunk as much as it can, you'll find that what you're eating is enough.'

'But I've got no energy. It's hard to get up. It's hard to do anything.'

'I'm the strong one. You don't need to concern yourself with anything other than holding out. If something happens, if it's cold, if you're frightened or if an animal attacks us, I'll defend you. I'm your big brother. Try to sleep.'

'I don't want to sleep yet. I'm afraid to.'

'Why?'

'Because I have dreams… strange dreams. I dream about eating things that I shouldn't eat. I dream about Mother… My dreams are terrible…'

'You mustn't be afraid of dreams; they aren't real. They're thoughts that we have in our head and they get all mixed up, memories that we can't put into words. If you dream about eating things it means you're hungry, that's all. If you dream about flying it means you want to go home… Do you see?'

Small assents with a lift of his chin. His brother's words soothe him and he closes his eyes. With his last breath before falling asleep, he asks:

'And what does it mean if I dream of eating Mother?'

7

T HEY COMPLETE their first week in the well and hear a new sound.

Small wakes up in a daze, still seeing with dream-filled eyes, as if he were moving through a bank of fog. Even by day the night rules in his pulse and a crepuscular stillness casts a haze over everything. His brother is breathing deeply. The sound comes back, closer now, bringing with it a tremor that reaches all the way down to the boys' earthen beds.

'Hello?' says Small, unsticking his dry mouth. 'Hello?'

When he speaks for the third time, Big calls out in chorus with him. Only just awake, he shouts according to a primal impulse, without knowing why. Both of them repeat the Hellos, the Helps, the We're heres. They clap, stamp their feet on the ground, howl. Then they fall quiet and listen for a response that might give some sense to their outbursts.

The wind is black and greets them with paws and breathy grunts, long like tongues. The brothers look at each other with eyes so wide it's as though they were trying to pop them out of their faces.

A pack.

'Wolves?' asks Small.

'I don't know. Did you hear growling?'

'No. Do you think they could be wolves?'

'They could be goats.'

'In the forest?'

'They could be lost. If they're goats, the shepherd might come after them.'

'And if they're wolves?'

'Then the shepherd won't come.'

The steps become more and more clear, and the sound of panting coming from the animals has taken over the night. Inside the well, the brothers' stillness is catching: the insects have stopped buzzing, the water has stilled in its tracks; at last, nature is silent. For a moment, the well slips its bonds and breathes like a home that the brothers don't want to lose. The siege appears to be a fleeting assault. A wash of calm crawls up the walls, stills the mouth of the well and extends beyond its sheer edges to where the baying creatures howl. They go quiet, and for a split second the forest settles in an implosion of peace.

Then, like an unearthed landmine, it hits them.

'Wolves!'

Snouts start to appear, sniffing out sweat and dirty flesh. The brothers know they reek, that their own excrement and bodies have given them away. The snouts are crowned with rows of jagged teeth, and above their slavering tongues, rounding off the image of the beasts, slitted eyes glisten, filled with night.

The boys open their mouths as if to shout, but don't.

The first of the wolves drops its head and eyeballs them, baring the roof of its mouth. It knows its prey is weak, that it's ailing and has no means of escape. There is constant movement at its sides. The pack circles the hole in a hunger dance. One of them extends its paws, threatening to pounce. It's not the only one. They seem to be considering ways of reaching their feed and retreating back into the forest. Another one prepares to launch itself into the well, the very idea of which leaves a long thread of drool dangling from its muzzle. But before it bends its legs a rock splits its head open and the dance breaks up.

'Get out of our house.'

The sound of bone cracking is followed by an authentic yelp, genuine pain. The animals protest and pace around, but the rocks keep hitting them all the same. They retreat.

'You got him!' says Small.

Over the next minutes a few of the wolves return to the hole, but without conviction. Most of them back off, regrouping several metres away where the rocks don't reach. Eventually, they leave.

'Can you hear them?'

'No. They've gone.'

'You frightened them.'

'Yeah. I frightened the wolves. With rocks!'

Small lets out an astonished laugh, still gripped with fear.

'Let's sleep for a while. They won't come back. There are still a few hours till the sun comes up, and we have to preserve our energy. You go first. I'll stay awake a bit longer, just in case any of the bastards show their faces here again.'

Small thinks, he said 'bastards'. His brother has beaten the wolves. Tonight he'll sleep like few nights before, and it will be the last night, too, that he rests peacefully.

Big settles down in the middle of the well, rocks in either hand, and he doesn't take his eyes off the hole. Tonight he'll ask himself how he would fend off the wolves if they got out of the well, and the thought won't let him sleep. In his head terrible images will take shape of his brother's skin separated from the bone, of his own, ripped apart in a bloody ritual, his mind still alert to the sound of the beasts as they chew.

11

FOR FOUR DAYS the sun scorches the fields, dries the well, and marks the trees with great strokes of copper. The water that filtered through the earth turns first to sludge, then to clods of black sand. When there is nothing left to drink, the two brothers break their daily routine to suck on the roots that poke out from the walls until their mouths taste of coal.

'I'm not well,' Small says.

'It will rain.'

They know this land well, the motions of the sky under which they've grown up, the cloud cycles. They know that a ferocious sun this month heralds an imminent downpour. It will rain because it always rains when their skin starts to peel, and because the land seems to be governed by a mechanism of suffering that works against every one of nature's decrees. As such, the people here are tough in skin and character, and they meet the exigencies of the land with unbending patience, without demands or complaint. This, however, presupposes a rupture in their emotional communication, in their shows of affection and in the human contract of cohabitation. The brothers are living proof of it. They no longer look one another in the eyes or search for themselves in the other as they did in the early days. Displays of affection aren't called for in a world dictated by the need to survive. Love is like a vow of silence, where cruelties befitting a reptile, a prehistoric crocodile, are meted out freely.

'Do you love me?' Small asks.

'It will rain.'

By the time the sun sets on the fourth day of drought they have gone hours without drinking a single drop of water, and Big is showing signs of dehydration. Even his urine has dried up. A silent rage throbs in his temples and for a moment he wants more than anything in the world to strangle his brother, to put his hands around his neck so that his eyes pop out of their sockets and he can bite into them and suck out the white jelly, as if they were salt-water sweeties.

'Don't ask me any questions.'

'I haven't said anything to you.'

'Don't talk to me either.'

Small closes his eyes and thinks about rivers, lakes, puddles of rainwater that he could splash and dance and jump about in. He imagines torrential floods in all flavours: lemon clouds that release their juice over the meadows and marinate the livestock; deluges of sweet orange to swim and dive in with his mouth open, never drowning; hailstorms of purple grapes; supernatural ice melts; underwater meadows. He digs a hole in the darkest part of the shade and puts his head in up to his ears, in a place where the soil retains a cool cover of blackness and silence. And in this ostrich-like pose his mind elevates beyond the well and his thirst disappears, his brother disappears, the prolonged pain in his stomach disappears, and his breathing slows to the exact stillness of invisible things.

He burrows down deeper still.

His teeth are covered with earth as he opens his mouth to breathe in the thick air. Deeper. The oxygen barely reaches his lungs, and in this state of near breathlessness he is struck by a flash of lucidity, a grey thought sparks white, and sets off a chain of impossible links. Each of his doubts corresponds to a certainty, like a tide of small fires that course into a river of molten lava. He is no longer himself. Now it is not him suffering this slow death in the well. Now no longer a thirst to quench. Now no. At the heart of his discovery is a murderous act of selfishness, new levels of indolence. He lets himself be carried by the nothing, by the emptiness…

'Get out of there, you idiot!'

Big grabs his legs and heaves the weightless body of his brother who hasn't moved a muscle in minutes and is practically unconscious. He seems to be immersed in a hallucinatory dream and Big slaps him on the face to snap him out of it. Small comes around and opens his mouth like a fish out of water. His neck is encrusted with sticky sweat and he coughs up grainy clumps of earth, with his tongue covered in a carpet of yellow moss and stone shavings.

'You nearly suffocated! Have you lost your mind?'

'I'm sorry. I'm not feeling well.'

'I've told you, it will rain. It always rains. You have to hold on.'

A couple of hours later, Small realizes that the well is not a well, but a mortar, and his brother is nothing but a fruit stuffed with bones that he must pestle in order to extract its oil, like they do with olives. At first he uses rocks to bash him, but the process is slow and onerous. So he builds a blood mill operated by oxen that drag a shaft, which in turn rotates an enormous stone, and grinds the flesh and bone and entrails until they become a wet paste. He then collects it all in his brother's skull and invokes the rain, which appears in the form of a gushing tap; and from a mixture of the water and the paste he distils a dark liquid, so thick he can neither chew it nor drink it, but which nonetheless sates his thirst, his hunger, everything. And when it is all gone, he positions himself underneath the huge stone and spurs the oxen.

By nightfall their bodies have collapsed and they lie unconscious, covered by a blanket of earth. A tremor courses through Small's fingers. Something in his mind has broken beyond repair from the thirst and hunger. His pupils spin like blind carousels. They see a lawless palace celebrating the eve of his madness. Big is suffocating. His parched skin sticks to his flesh and his muscles shine out like a moon, swollen from the strain of their daily overexertion. He gargles in his dreams and nibbles the cracked flesh of his lips so that a trickle of blood leaks down into his throat, filling him up until he feels sick.

As death appears at the edge of the well, the storm breaks.

13

DURING THE FIRST HOURS of rain they drank non-stop. They played, squelching from one side of the well to the other, and hugged. They drank themselves full and rolled about laughing, the laugh that exists on the border between elation and desperation.

Afterwards, they sat out the downpour with their backs against the walls, cornered, enduring the curtain of rain with stoicism. Little rivulets of insects and soil and leaves formed at the edge of the hole and crashed down in vertical torrents on top of them. The black sky reflected in the deep pools at their feet, choked with clouds that expanded and contracted like the lungs of an ocean. They drank for drinking's sake, anticipating another drought, and stuck their heads in holes in the ground and lapped away at the springs formed by trickles of water.

It stopped raining two days after the storm reached them. By then, the well had turned into a bog and its walls had warped. Their legs sunk into the wet, fudgy ground, their clothes began to rot after the prolonged exposure to the damp, and the mud seeped into their testicles and limbs. Big had not been able to do his exercises, and Small, who imagined the well like a limp, sagging coffin, stopped collecting food. They didn't celebrate the clear sky or the heat of the sun because their numb muscles were still trembling, and because the rain shower had demanded a gruelling feat of resistance: no sinking, no drowning, no sleeping. The lack of food had begun to take its toll on their shrunken stomachs, in particular that of Small, who slipped into a feverish stupor.

As the sun starts to dry the earth and evaporate the water from the saturated soil, and the well floor firms up again, Big notices that his brother is suffering from some form of pulmonary condition. He coughs up green mucus, thick like jam, and his forehead is on fire. Big dedicates himself to the task of feeding him regularly, giving him cool water every hour, keeping his clothes dry and moving him away from the last puddles. Totally devoted to the care of his brother, he neglects both to feed himself and do his exercises. Small's fever, however, does not abate.

To see him like this, emaciated and ashen, with the ribs of a starved greyhound, his fingers blue and forehead blazing, sick from the cold and from the phlegm, fills Big with an aching sadness. Small is a cut of barely breathing meat, settled in fitful sleep from which, every now and again, he wakes up in paroxysms of rage or of weeping and shouts garbled phrases. Big feeds him with perseverance and revulsion, but he feels a new affection when he lays him out in the sun and watches him stretch his limbs.

'You can't leave. You made a promise.'

At night, Big covers him with two layers of clothes to protect him from the frost. He curls up naked beside his small body and tries to warm it a little. He rubs him, kisses him, and holds him until he falls asleep.

'Maybe I do love you,' he says.

17

SMALL GOES ON DYING for days, and his brother goes on keeping him alive. As if they were playing.

Big feeds him the plumpest insects, the spongiest worms and the sweetest roots. He filters water through his shirt so that whatever he drinks is pure, crystal clear. He uses the coolest water from the morning to mop his brow, and the lukewarm water from the afternoon to wash his feet and hands and hair. When Small's breathing returns to normal and his fever abates, Big goes back to his physical exercises. Push-ups, sit-ups, squats. His head becomes drenched with sweat, and during these hours he stops thinking about his brother's illness; he escapes the well, charges across fields and dells and goes back. He ensures that justice is done. More than the hunger and the sun, it is the loneliness that ages him. It transforms his adolescent face into one belonging to a deeply wounded man—a man just back from a civil war or prison, his figure bent by the burden of so much toil and privation, and his big hands marked with new lines, calluses that he couldn't erase even if he wanted to. He talks to his brother like never before:

'When we go home we'll eat meat.'

He cooks him some dishes that they've tried once or twice, and others that he doesn't know, but can imagine. Cream of sun-blushed poppies with a few wild nuts and diced banana. Rice pudding with pink cinnamon, the rind of a lemon, a dusting of cacao and the syrup of a custard apple. Roast sea lion with strawberries and cassava in the juice of a ripe orange and coconut milk. He explains in detail how to peel potatoes, the best way to cut onions so that they soften in oil without burning, how long it takes to brown the best cut of chicken or beef. Once or twice, Small wakes up and says something in an apparent flash of lucidity. The odd word, stray sentences.

'Laurel…'

And so Big devises lessons in botany and agriculture, comparing methods, recalling smells and shapes and tastes. When he doesn't know them, he invents the secret reasons behind the order of things: he improvises entire cities where the natives speak other tongues; he travels beyond the cliff's edge and encounters indescribable wonders. He talks to him about the twin moons of the North and the wandering trees of the South. He tells him about the starry doves that live in the deep lakes, of houses with eyes where windows should be, and which weep tears of wine when their owners leave. He tells him about how when his grandparents were children they endured great floods which forced them to move the entire town a few kilometres down the road; about the cemetery of giants that covers an entire continent; and about the part of the sky that you can touch because it buckled under its own weight at the other end of the earth. He constructs geographies, ways of life, and labyrinthine, fanciful maths. He invents multicoloured cereal, women with crystals for nails, and fabled miracles: clay that protects you from bad fortune; magical creatures that live in the walls and grant a thousand wishes to whoever finds them; rivers that part if you ask permission. When he senses that he's become a bore and has exhausted his imagination, he tells him true stories.

'Sometimes I think we aren't really brothers.'

'It was me who killed our dog. With a stone.'

'I'll die in here.'

At night they sleep very close to one another. The moon is nearly full and its white light forms a gaseous orb over the edges of the wood, the tree canopies and the paths. The fever starts to leave Small's body, and with it his cough and the shivers and phlegm. For the first time since the storm passed they surrender to exhaustion and rest, truly rest, without interruption. They sleep so deeply that they don't hear the footsteps moving towards the mouth of the well, or notice the figure that appears and watches them, or see it disappear to return to where it came from in total silence.

19

THE TWINKLE has returned to Small's eyes, and with it the strength to collect food, but he has been left with the wastes of the fever still inside him. He does everything indifferently, as if he no longer cared to eat, or speak or breathe. His voice has changed, too: it has become darker and deeper.

'Where are we?'

He looks with the eyes of an adult who has eaten a child and infected him with a hundred centuries of madness. From closer up you can see that his shining eyes bear the weight of a wall, a wall containing a spiral of berserk ideas that have ladder hands and a forest head. With those eyes he scans the enormous body of his brother, sensitive to small changes.

'Drink more water. You must be dehydrated,' says Big.

'The real water is outside. This water is a lie.'

Big has resumed his full regime of exercises. He has spent over two weeks repeating them and this, along with his limited diet, has caused his muscles to develop strangely; they are misshapen, somewhere between those of a half-starved man and a mastiff. He is aware of the strain he is putting his body under, and that if he had to run, his heart would barely hold out for two kilometres before collapsing. His training is reproducing an incredibly short muscular memory, a kind of corporal amnesia that stretches the limits between survival and progress.

'I'm tired of the well. I'm leaving,' says Small.

'OK.'

'You don't think I can?'

'No. I don't think you can.'

'In that case, I'll leave you here to rot,' says Small, and his brother looks at him and doesn't recognize him.

Hours go by and neither says a word: Big, dumbfounded by the newfound independence of his brother's tongue; Small, consumed by his own musings and becoming ever more miserable.

'You've hardly eaten today,' says Big. 'If you don't eat, you'll die.'

'I'm not hungry.'

'You should eat even if you aren't hungry.'

'I'll eat when I'm hungry. I'll drink when I'm thirsty. I'll shit when I feel like shitting. Like dogs do.'

'We aren't dogs.'

'In here we are. Worse than dogs.'

*

The last of the sun's strokes sweeps away from the well, taking all life's colour with it and bringing the monotony of their cohabitation into relief. Like when, in the middle of a dream, it is all revealed to be make-believe and waking up is a kind of cruel joke.

'Your head's still not right after the fever. Have something to eat and go to sleep. Tomorrow you'll feel better,' says Big, lying down.

Small doesn't move.

'I think I've got rabies,' he says.

'No. You don't have rabies yet.'

Small looks at him lovelessly, and asks:

'Then what is this anger I can feel inside?'

'You're becoming a man,' says Big.

23

'TODAY, I'M GOING to teach you how to kill.'

For people like you and me, the first thing is anger. With no anger we will never find the necessary courage to take a life. There are other people who observe different impulses, who have grown up around unimaginable violence and look at you from inside caverns that you cannot even imagine. For those people, living is the well. You can't kill them, and if you confront them, they'll finish you off. You and me aren't like that. We require anger. A restless anger that won't let you stop, which bubbles under the skin, making your muscles shake; an anger that is black on your insides, but on the outside starts to turn you red, until you look like a burn victim who can't find his place in the world. You must charge yourself up with reasons to hate, despise whatever you see around you and, what's more, convince yourself that this anger is necessary. When you're full, don't hold it inside: release it, let it out into the world, shake it from your fingers, shout, run, burn the branches of trees, dig holes until your nails bleed, punch doors and walls and any other thing made by the hands of men. And before you collapse, exhausted, stop. Take a breath. Say nothing. For a few seconds, hold on to that last drop of anger in you; let it glisten at the corner of your mouth like a kiss about to fall. Exhale, feel your ribs rise and fall. Regain calm. Look at the destruction, your raw knuckles, the holes you've torn open with them. Feel the silence; how all matter, in its shock, has ceased to move; how the things around you no longer make a sound, the wood doesn't creak, the wind doesn't blow. It's the same silence that will one day occupy earth, when men decide to end it all and we witness the end of time. And it's the silence that you'll live with, too, every waking hour, while inside the anger transforms into its exact opposite.

Calm. This is the second thing. You must spend three days—not a day more or less—guarding the secret beginning to reveal itself inside of you. You must move like a bird, not touching the ground, and speak in a quiet voice so as not to disturb a single blade of grass. Try not to have any contact with anyone and go to bed early. And at all times—don't forget—remember that scarlet drop that you held back, think about it taking on the most horrifying forms in your body, until it becomes plumper and larger. Talk to it as if it were your disease, insult it, imagine the worst cruelties you could inflict, and subject it to your heart's desires so that it bleeds like a wound and oozes giant monsters. Live as if its presence weighed down on your back, be incapable of loving or admiring beauty. Note how loyalty squirms about

43

in your stomach and how an enormous void contaminates everything you touch. Finally, on the third night of this unbearable calm, when you take yourself off to sleep, take a deep breath, feel that breath move around your rotten insides, and let the calm engulf you. Let your disease lace you with poison like a spider's legs. Let the drop spread through your veins, showering you with razor-sharp stones. Let it cut you to the marrow with one foul slash. And then, sleep. And then, dream.

The last thing is will. The morning of the crime you won't be able to eat for the terrible dreams that will have plagued you. You'll do everything under the spell of a dazzlingly brutal violence, but a bubble of uncertainty will rove in circles around you, as if you were afraid to drink water for fear of breaking the glass. Don't worry. Take each step as it comes, feel your feet open up dark trenches along the bends of your soul, advance as if the earth turned and looked you directly in the eyes. And when at last, starved and terrified, you face your enemy, honour your resolve with the killing. Be quick, ferocious. Don't cause pain other than with your look. Give them a just, worthy death.

Killing, the act of killing, the force of your hands around the neck or the exact place where the knife sinks in, this can't be taught because it's already understood. Blades, firearms, sticks or stones, it's all the same. But remember that as men we must be there, watching as the light in their eyes goes out, living the crime at close range. We kill in seconds because we don't know any other way to kill. We're direct, impatient. Don't hesitate: it's your soul that will decide the precise movement, and once the deed is done you will be as great as all the great men who inhabited the earth before you.

These are the things you must know.

Small, who during the first few lines of the monologue didn't move, has set about sketching each of the concepts, drawing up symbols on the walls and the well floor which only he can make sense of, using his fingers and elbows like palette knives to translate these new teachings. He howls with wild abandon, testing out new sections of his brain with each revision of those terrible maps. The architecture of an unknown pleasure makes him drunk to the point of retching; it transports him to an archipelago of poisonous islands that roar like sea monsters. Shaken by earthquakes, he scans his wicked city again and again, memorizing it like a creed to which you give yourself with total devotion. He amends any miscalculations with the correct formulae and pales, horrified, before the flames spreading like wildfire through his childhood. Big observes him, satisfied.

At dusk the breeze and the water start to slowly smooth away the tracks that Small has worked so hard to put down. Like a sleepwalker, tired but with the conviction of someone who remembers everything, he decides that for the rest of his life he will carry writing paper and pencils, ink, quills, old books; tools that will allow him to attest for all time the miracles of his enlightenment. To translate the unpronounceable.

29

I MPRISONED NOW for an entire lunar cycle, hunger and desperation have broken both communication and their sanity. Big gets on with his exercise plan. Meanwhile, Small has descended the last steps of madness into a cellar devastated by hallucinations. He hums to himself repeatedly: popular songs whose lyrics he twists, making them obscene. He gives absurd speeches, which his brother has stopped listening to, whether out of boredom or a feeling of wretchedness.

'I think no one hears our cries because they mistake us for animals. You and I haven't noticed till now, but for days we have been talking like pigs. Tomorrow we'll shout in Latin. So they understand us.'

On other occasions he remains in silence for hours until an idea or rational thought snaps him out of it and compels him to shout out odd words, barely human sounds, nonsense poems.

'Today might be the eve of my self.'

Skeletal, unmoving and shamefully underfed, he cannot collect food like before, and now his brother undertakes this role, with the determination of a father. A sensation of bestiality governs them. The hunger in Small's stomach is so intense it rumbles like thunder and Big plugs his ears with two lumps of clay, modelled from earth and damp weeds, so as not to hear him. He only removes the earplugs for a couple of hours a day in the hope of hearing any noise in the forest that might signal help. But every night, driven half mad by the scandal going on in his brother's intestines, he puts them back, visibly saddened. He knows that with the earplugs in not only does he smother Small's voices, but also that crusted layer of guilt that he carries, and which eats away at him.

Small asks unnecessary questions:

'Why are we here?'

'Is this the real world?'

'Are we really children?'

Big never answers.

31

'YOU SHOULD KNOW, brother, that I am the boy who stole Attila's horse to make shoes out of his hooves, and in that way ensure that wherever I set foot the grass would no longer grow. The vilest of men fear me, as they fear the scourge of the gods, because I dried out their land and their seed in my vast wanderings across the world.'

'Did you do it alone?'

'With the Huns.'

'Who are the Huns?'

'Attila's soldiers. When he died many of them tore pieces of flesh from themselves. I'm also missing pieces of flesh, only you can't see because they're missing from the inside.'

Big sighs and puts his earplugs back in. His brother has fallen into one of his trances, more frequent of late, in which he doesn't seem to know who he is or where he has come from. The night before he spoke for a long time about human nature, explaining that men were marine beings before becoming land animals; he argued that for this reason it is important to look at the sea, because in doing so mankind can return to the origin of its species.

Later he took it upon himself to describe in the finest detail how certain feelings appear as he sees them in his mind. He arrived at some unbelievable conclusions, such as: the structure of hate is pyramidal and rotatory; or that boredom has a viscous inconsistency. Last thing before going to sleep he announced that every number could correspond to a word, and that one day he would be capable of expressing himself only through numbers. Those hellish monologues were unbearable for Big, since they confirmed the enormous, likely irreparable damage caused to his little brother by the fevers and deprivation.

'At first my feet hurt. I had to scoop out the insides of the hooves with a spoon and later stick them together with strips of black hide so that when I walked my feet could bend. They smelled like the shell of a dragon's egg, or like the skull of an idol. And they hurt my feet a lot, so much so that my heels bled and the nails came away from my toes. But when I got used to it I began to walk all over wearing the hooves, and I crossed entire lands that later turned to deserts. People ran away from me and I was happy. When I covered the same ground twice it went black. I walked for years all over the world, and you could see the footsteps of my pilgrimage from the sky like a dreadful wound that wouldn't heal.

'Then I wanted to find out what might happen if, instead of walking in my shoes over paths and forests, I walked over people. I chose a camp where everyone was sleeping and I jumped from body to body in a game of bouncy hopscotch. At first nothing happened, but later they began to wake up, screaming and vomiting, their skin shrivelling up like grapes which left yellow stains on the floor. Their bodies turned brown and red. It looked like a poor man's rainbow: lustreless, born out of a candle and a puddle of urine. I felt important, like a painter. I noticed that the adults dried out quicker than the children, and that the children didn't weep when they saw death approaching, but received it peacefully, understanding it. I continued along my way, crushing towns and races, and I know that an entire language fell out of use because I jumped excitedly—excited enough to nearly cause myself an injury—on the last man who spoke it.

'When I grew old, a few years ago, I took off my shoes for the first time since I was a boy, and I saw that my feet were still small. They were clean, unmarked; they even smelled good. I placed the shoes in a golden box, which I placed in a silver box, which I placed in a bronze box, and I buried them in a well in the forest that is half a day's distance from my old house, and in there I left two of my children so that nobody could ever take them away.'

37

S OME NIGHTS Big finds he cannot sleep, whether for the nightmares tangled up with painful memories, or because of his quiet dreads, fuelled by the forest's sounds and the thick air of the darkness. Having now spent over five weeks in the well, insomnia is just another routine in the small and ridiculous perimeter of his life. It's natural, he thinks, for men to lose the ability to sleep when their world is becoming choked up. That's why revolutions by injured peoples take place at night, like plagues.

In restless moments like these, he lies on his back and counts the stars. Alert to any little sign of flight or breath or moan, he has no other means to bring on sleep. Nor does he want to disturb his brother's rest; fragile, like the skeleton of a butterfly.

And so it is that in the distance, with ears so wide they could hold an ocean, he hears branches bending, then the sound of fumbled walking through the forest shrubs and potholes, followed by a few hovering steps on tiptoe which, on arriving at the mouth of the well, stop and turn—first one then the other, agile and devious like fox feet—edging towards a lookout onto a cage of children.

Big does nothing. He doesn't move, or speak, or breathe. He just listens so that he can fix his eyes on the exact spot. His pupils are so large they could make out the very eyelids of a crow as it circled the moon. He knows where to look:

There.

A head appears and looks down inside the well.

Big knows the features of that face.

Someone returns his gaze.

Then, no one.

Big remains silent, though his breathing has quickened and his heart is pumping acid. He locks his jaw hard, grinding his teeth and making the nerves in the gums between his teeth ring. It's a pleasant kind of pain, which suppresses the scream building up inside him. A scream like a lump of food in the stomach after a heavy meal.

And willing the wind to carry consonants and vowels across the night, and for his words to penetrate further than any scream could reach, he whispers:

'I'm going to kill you.'

41

B<small>IG HAS HIS CLAY EARPLUGS</small> in and he can't hear the shouts coming from his brother, but he senses a change of direction in the air streams around him. When he turns around he finds Small scratching his arms, eyeballing him like a lunatic and opening his mouth in desperation. Big takes out the earplugs and listens:

'Dungo sat! Dungo was goswun!'

Big doesn't understand. He thinks it must be another of his brother's deliriums and goes to put his earplugs in again. Small, though, stops him with a shove and goes on shouting, pointing at his throat with trembling hands.

'Nu wemee? Wemee bunder? Dungo was menhaman! Menitimo!'

The urgency in Small's voice is a sign that something is not right. It isn't a delirium. It's as if he had just learnt to speak. Like when one cuts a piece of paper into strips and tries to put them back together but can't form a rectangle, only a misshapen page.

'Cunnard burds, un cunnard fesis, nemnay! Nemnay fa wampus! Saired!'

After so many weeks listening to Small's crackpot mono-logues Big can't help but see the irony in the strange process that has overcome him, and for the first time in a long while he sees a funny side, and has to discreetly stifle a laugh.

'It's all right. I'll mend the wampus for you, don't worry. The wampus is under control.'

And the second he utters the phrase he explodes in a snort of laughter, loud like a collapsing quarry. And just like a landslide he can't stop it, not even when he sees the dagger eyes his brother is throwing him.

'Forgive me. I'm sorry. Don't get angry. It's just the wampus…'

And again he bursts out laughing, beside himself now, out of control, the fits feeding themselves on more fits in an endless cycle of wampus. He laughs so hard that he falls to his knees clasping his middle, his belly, his jaw and his throat hurting. Small, too, is beside himself, but for other reasons: rage, puzzlement, fear; he is seized by a new kind of loneliness, and for a few seconds drastic thoughts race around his head: he might never speak properly again, might never be able to write or leave his mark. He might box his brother to death, stamp over his spine until it crunches underfoot, and leave him paralysed. He might never be able to say goodbye, or say I love you, or throw insults. Pointing his finger at Big, still on the ground on all fours, he screams:

'Raturl! Filffif doan gon hurtul! Gon hurtul dop unterme! FOTON DUCRUZZER!'

Like adding fuel to the fire. Small's accusing finger, the indignant look on his face, and the insult that the words 'foton ducruzzer' are clearly meant to represent are too much for Big. Doubled up in stitches he tries to find some words of comfort for his brother. Small launches a useless assault, hitting him with a few weak blows, and Big makes an effort to calm him down.

'Don't hit me. I'm sorry. I'll stop laughing now.'

Small hits him again.

'Stop it! I've told you I'm sorry. Let me get up.'

Small makes as if to throw another punch, but instead he says:

'Yefonk!'

Big suppresses a fresh attack of the giggles.

'Yes, I fonk. Don't worry. I know what's happening to you.'

'Luno wonsat neme? Nenay.'

'You're suffering from a kind of speech defect. It's not serious. It will pass.'

'Surro?'

'Yes, surro. Believe me. You have to rest and try to relax. You can't keep thinking all the time like you have these last days.'

'Nime der ra. Me ra. Holenark fut inun wound ma vote. Shelling, or darjung.'

'I know, I know.'

Big puts his arm around Small, who receives the display of affection with a shudder, then bursts into tears, letting his trembling body fold into his brother's. Between sniffles, Small says:

'Amam cor.'

A few hours later, Small is practising speaking under his breath, like a slave learning how to write in secret with old exercise books. He thinks 'brother' and his mouth utters 'furo'. He thinks 'donkey' and says 'kenko'. Exasperated, he decides to start by repeating the simplest words, those with a single syllable. He thinks: 'sun'.

'Crun.'

'Faa.'

'Sato.'

'Sot.'

'Sonn.'

'Sonn.'

'Sun.'

He can hardly believe it as he speaks the word. He repeats it, louder:

'Sun.'

'Sun!'

'SUN!'

He erupts with joy. Getting to his feet he cries 'SUN'

and sploshes around the well with his arms raised, clenching his fists and his eyes, 'SUN' and 'SUN' and 'SUN'. Big, who until that point was sleeping peacefully, is wrenched from his dream by the revelling gladiator.

'What about the sun? It's already night time!' he says, his eyes bleary. Small just smiles, satisfied.

43

OVER THE FOLLOWING DAYS the aphasia gradually fades. Small can pronounce the simplest words without a problem, but those that are more complex still defeat him, especially when he tries constructing elaborate sentences or speeches. An inexact means of communication, which must recover the very kernels of understanding.

'Hunger.'

'You'll eat what is strictly necessary.'

And yet, Small is right. Food is becoming scarce, almost certainly as a result of the brothers' continued plunder of every inch of the well as they forage for roots and insects, small eggs and maggots. What's more, Big's decision over the distribution of the food means that Small can barely move, and he spends all day prone on the floor like a vegetable, growing deep ulcers between his buttocks and on his legs. Although skinny and pale, Big retains a certain vigour, the result of a more balanced diet and the obsessive repetition of his exercises. He knows that in these deprived conditions his brother's time is running out, so in the hope of finding something for him to eat he sinks his hands into the last crevices of the well, delving shoulder-deep into the hard earth. He spends hours like this, then comes across an earthworm, a significant portion of which he loses as he pulls apart the earth to reach it. He hands the worm over and his brother bolts it down without saying a word or moving anything but his tongue.

Small savours the earthworm and imagines he is sucking on a magic pill. There and then he develops superhuman powers: he can fly like an eagle, be as strong as ten men; he is capable of understanding every language on the planet. He decides to leave the well and starts flapping his arms. He lifts up off the ground, one, two, three hands high. He comes across fresh roots. His brother becomes small. And just as his head emerges and he sees the full magnitude of the forest, a rough stake jabs him out of nowhere and he plummets down. He gets up, in pain, but now more sticks appear, walloping him in the nape of his neck and on his arms, and again he falls. His pride is injured now, and he rises up, carried on a typhoon of hate, faster and faster, and at the summit he is showered by a hundred, a thousand sticks that strike him like the keys of a mute organ. He zooms about, blindly smashing into them—a mosquito trapped inside a swarm. Yet, he doesn't fall. The blows keep coming and he doesn't fall. In the end, with nothing to lose, he decides to test whether, among the various gifts that the earthworm bestowed on him, immortality is one of them, and he declares war. An armed mob confronts him. You have no right to fight, they tell him. Next thing, Small attacks.

In the afternoon Big gives up and sits down next to Small. The hunger remains. One of the brothers struggles to remove the latent idea of cannibalism from his head. The minutes slide over them as if the well were a courtyard of abandoned statues in the vault of mother earth.

A plump bird lands at their feet, cawing.

47

'FILTHY SON OF A BITCH.'

The bird was dead within the two or three seconds it took the brothers to surround and jump on top of it. Driven by his hunger, it was Small who moved fastest and clutched the bird by its neck, rendering useless any effort by the animal to fly off again. He grasped so tightly with his forefingers and thumbs that by the time the bird had suffocated its head was practically separate from its body.

'You little pile of shit.'

It was then that the problems began. Small's first instinct was to sink his mouth into the belly of the bird, but his brother stopped him, throwing him off with a hefty shove. Small fell flat on his back, switching from jubilation to shock, from shock to anger.

'Miserable fucker.'

While blocking his brother's onslaught, Big tried to explain to him that they would not eat the bird right then. Their shrunken stomachs wouldn't be able to digest the raw meat of the animal, or its bile and intestines. They would have dreadful stomach pains, would vomit virtually at the first mouthful and, without a doubt, what little they might manage to digest and pass through their intestines would come straight out the other end in the form of torrential diarrhoea.

'Bastard.'

Small had other ideas. According to him, after having eaten insects and larvae and worms for weeks, his stomach could accommodate the raw meat perfectly well, kidneys and all—if the bird even had kidneys—and in spite of the fact that he never would have eaten kidneys at home, because they were repulsive. The only reason his brother wouldn't let him taste even a morsel of the bird, he maintained, was because of the rigorous division of food he had decreed way back on that day.

'Stingy arsehole.'

The right way to eat it, continued Big, in spite of his brother's mounting rage, was to cook it. That is, to roast it or bake it. But the lack of utensils as well as the humidity inside the well prevented them from making a fire. And without fire it was impossible to cook anything. Nor could they smoke it, or salt it, or marinate it in vinegar or oil. There was no way around it.

'If you died now, I'd piss on your corpse.'

But there was one option. An option that meant eating. And eating more than the sum of the last days' fare put together. The problem, however, was that they would have to wait a day or two, maybe three, before trying a morsel. That is: go on starving with the banquet laid out before them.

'Shit-eater, deformed son of a whore.'

They needed to wait for the bird to decompose so that the flies, blowflies and maggots would come out to gorge on it. Small protested vehemently. Where was the justice in letting a load of bugs have their fill on the food that he'd been forbidden to eat? His brother explained that if they left the animal out in the air, without burying it, the decomposition process would be quicker, and that they could eat the flies and the maggots, hundreds of maggots, and that they would have food for days. What's more, food they were used to and which would sit well with them.

'You're a little sack of shit.'

Though in no way in agreement, Small had to bow down to the superior strength of his brother, who guarded the dead bird with his whole body as if he were defending a fortress. Only once Small was sound asleep did Big succumb to the lightest of slumbers and rest. There was no doubt in his mind that, given half a chance, his brother would pounce on the bird and devour the whole thing down to its bones.

'I'd like to rip your rotten face from your head.'

If the first night was hard, the day after was even worse. There were no civilities, no good mornings or routines, just unbridled, nasty violence. Tension and silence kept a pressure cooker of unease bubbling away: Big in one corner,

Small in another, the bird between them. The stench coming off the animal seemed to intensify the fury with which they watched one another. It was as if the clock had stopped, like dead time in a battle.

'Sheep-shagger, son of a boar and a monkey.'

When a few flies began to buzz around the corpse, Big ate every one and looked at his brother with a triumphant smile. When a few more appeared, Small refused to eat them, despite the fact that Big was managing, painstakingly, to catch them and invited him to do the same. Your pride will kill you, he said, to which Small replied with insults.

'Dickhead, idiot, freak.'

It didn't take long for the maggots to creep out from under the wings, like roving tumours. The first ones were small, then succulent, ring-bound bodies sprouted out of the rotten flesh, moving in and out of its orifices. Big's face lit up with joy. He caught one between two fingers as it pushed its way out of the bird's neck. He put it in his mouth and felt an explosion of liquid and jelly as he chewed. He couldn't recall having eaten anything so tasty in his life.

'Screw your dead family.'

He ate a few more while Small watched and hurled insults at him contemptuously. Once Big had had his fill, he took the biggest maggot he could find and offered it to his brother.

'Eat. It's really good.'

'I don't want to eat your shitty maggots.'

'They taste like chicken. And they're not cold.'

'Fuck you. Fuck off and die.'

'You are the one who will die if you don't eat.'

'Which means I won't have to see your scummy face.'

'Eat.'

Small is so hungry that he can no longer control his body. He baulks, but puts out his hand, into which Big places a colossal maggot, as juicy as a ripe apple.

'Abuser. Nasty pig. I hate you.'

Finally he eats. He chews the gelatinous fibre of the maggot a dozen times and the bitter juice that oozes from it dances on his tongue. He drools like a hungry dog. It doesn't taste of chicken: it's better than chicken. He bursts into tears like the little boy that he was.

'You're the best. I love you. I love you.'

The feast goes on all night.

53

'IF I WANTED TO,' says Small, stretched out on his back with his arms open like a crucified man, 'I could change the order of things. I could move the sun so that it fell on us in the middle of the afternoon and that way we wouldn't be cold after our nap. I could go and collect the old smells from the village and fill our noses with freshly made bread, apple turnovers, chocolate. I could build a spiral staircase from inside the well right up to the trees and then bend it back so we can hop off it again without hurting ourselves. I could turn water into milk and insects into chickens and roots into liquorice. But I don't want to. I don't want to do anything. It's enough to be here and for the universe to keep turning around me. It's what happens to us who are dead.

'The living… the living are like children: they play at dying. I lived among tough men who weren't scared of death, and with smart men who cheated it, and with weak men who let themselves be dragged along by it, but none of them understood the minuteness, the insignificance of a world devoted to that cause. I don't understand it. I didn't understand it till now… Look at me… Three big steps. This is all the distance I can cover before the walls cut me off. Three big steps. My world is as small as theirs; it's a jaw that locks on to me and salivates, diluting me, as if it wanted to erase me, and my own battle is reduced to staving it off. Is this it? Must men live within walls with no windows or doors? Is there something beyond this life while life goes on? There is, brother, there is! I know it! Because in my head, in here, where no one can see, nothing can hold me back. It's a land without walls, without wells, just for me. And it's real because it's changing me; the pain it gives me is different, the days are never-ending. Time is a crossroads nailed between my eyes. My whole childhood will happen tomorrow, I'll take my first steps tomorrow, I'll say my first word tomorrow. It's a glorious feeling, when summer arrives… You think I'm ill? Ignoramus! You think I haven't proved myself? I know very well that you pay no heed to my words, but this doesn't make them any less true. If only you were able to see what I see, this darkness of days. But also this inexplicable warmth, so close to love… Don't you see it? Don't you feel the liquid engulfing us as if we were foetuses? These walls are membranes and we are floating within them. We move around in anticipation of our long-awaited delivery. This well is a uterus, you and I are yet to be born, our cries are the agonies of the world's birth.'

*

Big has been listening to his brother in silence, barely understanding a word of what he says. Every day it gets harder to follow him, and he has the feeling that in the end he will be left behind, that Small will keep moving on his journey and won't look back. Then he says:

'When you were born the doctor couldn't get there in time and it was me who pulled you from Mother's belly. The kitchen was filled with blood and your pig-like squeals. I didn't know how to make you be quiet, so I put one finger in your mouth for you to suckle on. Mother was asleep, and after a while you fell asleep too, but you went still and you were so tiny and your chest wasn't moving. I thought you were dead. That I'd poisoned you with my thumb, or who knows what. I was so scared… I screamed at you, too much, and when you woke up I carried on screaming, and you must have thought that the world was a horrible place. I couldn't sleep for weeks, for months.'

'Why are you telling me this?'

'Because I want you to understand that I am not afraid of dying, I don't base my life on the knowledge that one day it will all end. There are times when life presents circumstances where the only recourse is a radical move, an extraordinary sacrifice, and I can accept that. What I couldn't bear, though, would be to see you grow up in a wasteland, like this well; a place to die with no peace,

69

all because of the apathy of civilization. A cemetery in which to wither, like a flower that won't ever help the land to grow. It is the thought of you dying that makes the world so small.'

59

S MALL HAS NAMED himself Inventor and he organizes cultural activities for his brother, although really he does it because he cannot stop imagining.

He has perfected what he has called 'osteo-vegetable music', which is what comes from hitting certain bones with dry roots. He rehearses on his own body, above all with his knees, hips, torso and collarbone. But what he'd really love would be to somehow rotate his head and arms and rock out on his spine. His extreme boniness makes him look like a misshapen neighbourhood made up entirely of street corners, and this affords him an inordinate range of obscure, high-pitched sounds which come together as a tune when he strums his tendons and thumps his stomach and chest. The result is a series of concerts with a hard, repetitive bass line, but which boast brief flashes of harmony so that, skeletal origins aside, one can appreciate a certain musicality. Apart from the symphonies, Small takes particular pleasure from his elaborate overtures, where with great ceremony he takes up position—to play himself—and explains the contents of the works with such unfeigned titles as 'Kneecap and Ribs Song', 'Hungry Fingers' and 'At Night a Cranium'.

He also organizes outings to The Well Space, home to various temporary art exhibitions. He dedicates a lot of time to finger-painting on the walls: generally abstract pieces embellished with stones, roots and rotten leaves. Unfortunately he can only draw one or two works in the space available to him, and in order to make room for new installations he is obliged, much to his sadness, to delete the old ones. Had it been possible to preserve every one of them and arrange them chronologically, an astute observer would have picked up on his painstaking narration of life inside the well, a kind of pagan Stations of the Cross. *Wolves Smelling Men*, *The Arrival of the Sea*, *First Worm*, or *The Bird of Virtuous Death* were acclaimed works and only just missed forming part of The Well Space's permanent collection.

Energy levels permitting, his creativity extends to another kind of pursuit, one that requires greater exertions: gestural theatre, folk dances, human sculptures and contortionism, activities that Big also takes part in on occasion. But the privation of recent times has reduced the number of festivals, much treasured when they do go ahead.

At the end of the day's line-up, Big spends a few minutes applauding, whistling and hear-hearing like a doting public. Afterwards, if he finds Small in good spirits, he calls for an encore and bows in reverence until he gets one, at which point they fall about laughing at the unintended variations on the show, always unrepeatable.

A few hours later, famished and exhausted, they can hardly remember what they have done, seen or heard.

'Who are you?' asks Small.

'You know who I am,' answers Small.

'How did you get here?'

'The same way as you. Falling into the well.'

'Where have you been these past weeks? I haven't seen you before.'

'I kept quiet.'

'And now you want to talk?'

'Let's.'

Big is snoring like a wild boar.

'Am I going to die?' asks Small.

'Yes. One day. Does that worry you?' answers Small.

'Sometimes. When I've got things to say it scares me to think I don't have time to say them. My brother thinks I hallucinate, but he's wrong. It's sort of an emergency.'

'You're not special in that regard.'

'Yes I am. I think things the others don't think. I see

things the others don't see, or if they see them they can't interpret them correctly.'

'You speak as if you know the truth.'

'No. I speak as if I were tired of being wrong.'

'And you're not wrong anymore?'

'No. It's everything else that's wrong. This well, the walls, the forest, the mountains. I've been confused for a long time, but I'm OK now.'

'You don't look OK.'

'I'm going to die. I've never been better.'

'Will we get out of the well one day?' asks Small.

'You, yes. In twenty-eight days,' answers Small.

'And my brother?'

'The young boy sleeping over there will never get out. His bones will turn to dust here in this hole. Someone must die in order for you to live; you must know that by now.'

'I don't want him to die. He's being strong for me.'

'Many will be strong for you. You will show your gratitude when the time comes. To your brother, too.'

'I don't know how I ever could… I've got nothing to give them. There is a hole where other things should be.'

'You can't fight that. Nobody will be able to fill that hole, that hunger you feel every day. You can't sate yourself.'

'It's like a prison sentence.'

'I suppose it is. I'm sorry.'

'Don't be sorry. I had options, but I chose this path.'

'And what do you think you will find at the end?'

'It doesn't matter. Maybe a punishment, or a reward. Maybe there'll be pain, nothing but pain, a searing white pain that will leave me blind. I don't care. Life is wonderful, but living is unbearable. I'd like to pare down existence. To pronounce over a century one long, inimitable word, and for that word to be my true testament.'

'A testament for whom?'

'For whoever understands it.'

'Do you think I will be remembered?' asks Small.

'Perhaps by your contemporaries, by your generation,' answers Small.

'That's not enough. I don't know if I belong to any generation: none of my loved ones are my age. I will be remembered by all, until not one man remains on the earth.'

'And why should you be remembered?'

'For what I know. For what I am going to do. For surviving the well. For my visions. Because my words are new. Because I am big.'

'No, you're not. You're Small.'

'That is only a name.'

67

S MALL HUMS SOFTLY to himself like a ventriloquist's
dummy, while Big urinates blood and thinks that his
time is up. A red puddle splashes the earth before being
soaked up into it. Big sees it as his body's final warning.
Perhaps he's pushed it too far. Or perhaps his kidneys were
always going to pack up today, at this very moment, even if
he had been living at home and eating normally. He covers
the blood with brown earth and smiles.

'Today,' he says, 'I feel wonderful.'

The absent look on his brother's face makes him question whether Small, like him, is haemorrhaging blood and
not saying so. Looking at his paper-thin body it seems
impossible that it would survive blood loss. Then again,
over these weeks he has shown that his desire to stay alive
is great enough to survive even the gravest illnesses. That
small, gaunt thing has battled against hunger, thirst, fevers,
the cold and heat, and although his mind has begun to
desert him, his spirit stands firm.

He envies Small's indolence and self-absorption, and all
the shades of grey that his world seems to contain.

'Want to play?'

Small perks up all of a sudden.

'Yes. What shall we play?'

'A guessing game.'

'I spy with my little eye something beginning with en.'

Small pulls an intrigued face and strokes a non-existent beard, squinting his eyes. He knows his brother, and, given that there aren't too many options within their line of vision from the bottom of the well, he knows which word he is thinking of. But he enjoys playing, and the best thing about the game is the game itself.

'Necessity!'

'No.'

Words beginning with en pile up in his head, all of them a product of his captive condition. He decides to stretch the rope a little more, to test his brother's resistance.

'Necrosis!'

'No.'

'Niche!'

'No!'

He loosens the knot a fraction: his brother is clearly losing the will to go on.

'Nothing!'

'No.'

'It's really difficult. Give me a clue.'

'OK… You can see it, but you can't touch it.'

Now is the moment of joy. He can't put it off any longer.

'Nightfall!'

'Yes! Well done!' bursts out Big with an enormous smile.

'Again!'

'Something beginning with… ar.'

Small admires the simplicity of his brother. It must be easy to make decisions in a world with such radical contrasts, where everything is black and white. It must be easy to do the right thing.

'Rage!'

'No.'

Interred in a well, his brother sees roots. He cannot see anything else because he looks in the way that dogs look. It is that basic, that beautiful. A piece of meat and a few pats of his back would suffice to make him feel loved. Roots. For Small, there are entities more certain than those things he can touch.

'Reality!'

'No!'

Human Remains. Rations of insects. Red-Raw knees. Rebellions. Ravings. Routines. Rituals. Rot. The game could be a lot more fun if only his brother understood. He throws him a bone out of the goodness of his heart.

'Rocks!'

'Warmer!'

'Am I close?'

'Very. Go on!'

Nor does he want his brother to think him an idiot.

'Roots!'

'You got it!'

'Cool!' Small hoots exaggeratedly. 'Now it's my turn.'

'OK, but none of those abstract words. Only things that can be seen.'

'Agreed.'

'I spy…' begins Small.

'I spy,' says Big.

'I spy with my little eye… Something beginning with… bee. With bee! With bee!' Small shrieks, looking down at the russet-coloured earth.

'LOCK UP ANY MAN in a cage,' says Small.

Give him a blanket, a feather pillow, a mirror and a photograph of the ones he loves. Find a way to feed him and then forget about him for a number of years. Under these conditions, in the majority of cases the end result will be a shell of a man, reduced to guilt, bent to the shape of a cage.

In exceptional cases, he goes on saying, the chosen subject will die, consumed by the slow wasting of his essential organs, or he will go insane watching his own reflection in the mirror. Or he will die of a terminal illness, which in any case he was fated to suffer.

On the other hand, for those subjects predisposed to rebel, those who can't ignore the call of their inquisitive spirit, prolonged captivity is impossible: lock up a rebel in a cage for a few years and he will either escape, commit a meticulously planned suicide making use of the objects he has at his disposal, or die carving up his own body into pieces small enough to pass through the bars. The real problem, though, is the way these dissenters—fertile by nature—breed and spread in our human conscience: when one dies, two occupy his place.

Given the above, imagine cages hanging from the ceilings of every café, bookshop, church, hospital, and, above all, every school, and imagine that at least one of those cages is inhabited by a subversive—a non-conforming, rebelling subject. Imagine the speeches of these twisted, concave bodies, incited by the crowds who surround their altar with their guilty consciences; what perverse, lucid public acts will they come out with during their reign. Imagine what will become of the inmate from a hospital, beautiful and sustained like a blue machine that pumps out memory, bearing witness to disease and corpses. Imagine the prisoner from a church, near blind, forced into a plaintive silence of prayer and worship. Imagine a wise man like a picked flower, drooping in the perfect position of the captive, taking off every winter with the first gust of wind that comes from the west!

Imagine…

Imagine I can forge the key to the cells. That we wait years, many years, and that afterwards, when the world is fully inured to hiding men behind the bars of a cage, when tradition and indifference require that all the lost souls, the coerced, the imprisoned become the product of a storage warehouse social system, a generation of domestic animals, a race made up of furniture and ancient mummies, and then, only then, we set them free.

And let them be like fire, the unconquerable summer of all winters.

The world would be ours, he ended, brother.

73

WHEN HE WAKES UP he thinks about how giving oneself up to hallucinations is not the same as when hallucinations prevail over sanity and finally break the soul. There's a difference in attitude.

'I have to get out of here,' says Small.

'You will. Very soon.'

'You don't understand. I have to get out of here now. I'm not well. I'm losing my mind.'

Small can pinpoint his real sickness. He knows that his organs have stopped fighting against starvation and the elements, that they will hold out no more than a few days, but his head will never recover. It hurts as if a bubble of gas were expanding in the centre of his brain, making the lobes press against his skull and hammering red-hot needles into his memories, into his ability to add and subtract, into the abyss out of which his words arise. If he could, he would cut up his bones into little splinters and let the brain matter slide out through his ears, letting him breathe.

The pain is so severe that Small curls himself up into

a ball in a corner of the well, massaging his temples with his fingers. He babbles like a newborn baby.

Big watches him nervously and tries to calm him down by rubbing his back.

'Hold on.'

A few hours later the situation has worsened. Small's jaw goes into spasm, he dribbles and he can no longer string full sentences together.

'Shiver... mind going...'

He doesn't want to eat, because he's not hungry. It's something else. Deep cracks open up in his thoughts and he can feel how the walls that contain them are beginning to collapse. He feels his reason plunging into a hole; waste collects at the smoking base and noxious fumes rise up and lacerate the chimney of his sanity. He is saying goodbye to reality. It is defeating him.

'I must hurry...'

Big can do no more than comfort him and trust that the exhaustion will overcome him and force him to rest. He is still not ready to take him out of the well. He needs a few more days; less than a week, maybe. He will only get one chance and he can't risk the effort of these last two months and a half, even if his brother is losing weight quicker than he can bear. It's torture to see him this way—destroyed, in the last agonies, like a city that's been flattened by a meteor—and he feels more shame still for feeling so strong in himself, for surviving with such dignity. But he can't pity him, not now. Not if he wants to keep his promise.

A fine rain numbs the night. Big places maggots in Small's mouth and pushes them right to the back of his throat to force him to swallow them. The boy takes them without fuss.

'Thank you, thank you,' he says.

'Don't thank me. Eat.'

'I'm somewhere far away…'

'I know. But I can still see you.'

'No… You can't.'

'I'm seeing you right now. I'm talking to you.'

'You aren't talking to me. I'm an echo.'

'Sleep, please. Don't talk anymore,' says Big with a quake in his vocal cords, despite himself.

'It's been weeks since it was me talking.'

To the nocturnal eyes of his brother, it looks like Small is wrapped in a black shroud, the scribbled sketch of a prehistoric child. He lifts him up and rocks him to the rhythm of a drifting boat. An ancient voice carries across a hundred generations and shakes them:

'*Sleep, my child, sleep. They say that life is good. They speak— let them speak!—, they know not what they say. Sleep, my child,* sleep. *Your day will come and you shall have the longest, sweetest rest. Sleep, my child, sleep. The gentle night is coming—for me, and then for you,'* Big sings, without thinking, without knowing what he says.

79

IN A FIT OF HYSTERIA Small scoops up several fistfuls of earth and eats them. Minute stones grind against his back teeth and the grit scratches the enamel, twisting his attempt at a smile into a grimace. It only takes a few seconds before he is bent double, vomiting a dark paste of soil and bile, but the smile still hangs from his face. He looks like he has risen from the dead.

'Beeerrrrggggg, beeerrrrrggggg,' he says.

Big doesn't know if it was an attack of hunger or an attempted suicide. Seeing how he smiles it seems more likely the upshot of a terminal mental breakdown. He knocks him cold when he goes to scoop up more earth and carry on eating.

Even unconscious he holds on to the crazed smile.

In the hours that follow, Small stirs a few times; momentary spasms of lucidness that alternate with heartrending cries, whimpers and incoherent monologues. He doesn't have a temperature; it's more like he has knocked his head and the impact has jogged his brain out of place, flipping it over. He spits continuously. His eyelids open and close like the wings of a fly, beating large pieces of coppery rheum that fall off then stick to his cheeks. An invisible leprosy is consuming him.

'Water,' he asks.

Big gives him a drink.

'I'm cold.'

Big lies down beside him and holds him with all of his body.

'I'm hot.'

Big undoes his brother's shirt, mops his collar and the nape of his neck with cool water, and then flaps his own to create a current.

'I'm dirty.'

Big takes down his brother's trousers, wipes his buttocks with damp earth and dresses him again.

'I'm scared.'

Big lifts him up in his arms, the way a groom carries his new wife, and rocks him. He weighs so little he could hold him in one hand.

'Kill me.'

83

IT IS A COOL DAWN. An invitation to go on sleeping, to sink back into the warm earth and let the forest's hum slowly stir the senses. The sun just about warms his toes, his ankles, his legs. It strokes his skin and makes his hair stand on end, but doesn't burn him. Flocks of birds chatter in the trees before flying off. Big is awake, but his eyes are still shut. He wants to draw out the bliss of his slumber, to let himself be towed by the undercurrent all the way to the shore. He knows that all pleasure will disappear when he opens his eyes to the sky and the walls of the well cover him with their heavy shadow.

His mind made up, he concentrates all his strength in one eye, then, at last, opens it, and the morning enters in like a spray of light, blinding him for a few seconds, drawing back the curtains in one stroke. The world spins.

Around him the bed of earth is all stirred up. He is still not completely awake. He yawns. He rubs his eyes to level his horizon. He yawns again. Something seems different. He blinks. He looks. Something is different.

Small is not there.

It feels like a lightning bolt is moving through him from his genitals all the way up to his heart, electrifying his organs, coursing through his cells. Small is not there. Adrenaline bursts into thousands of bubbles that dampen his stupor as if with a shower of metal, and leave him like a cat caught in acid rain. Small is not there. He turns his head this way and that in such a hurry that he looks without seeing and his brain can't retain the visual details of his surroundings. It's not possible, he thinks.

He breathes in. He looks again, this time taking his time. There are no footprints on the walls. There are no hand or tread marks. If his brother has escaped from the well, he will have had to do it by flying. He looks again. The soil on the ground has been turned over. He stops. There is a mound over in the corner, like a camel's hump. He hasn't seen it before. He moves closer. The bulge is a mountain formed out of layers of fresh soil. Behind it, a half-closed hole. Or half open.

In the time it takes for him to swoop down on the hole and start to haul up layers of soil, he has understood that his brother has spent the night digging a tunnel underneath the well. He screams as his arms sink and rise up again and his skin shreds, leaving his hands like red-hot trowels.

And he goes on screaming as his nails break off, flipping like snapped animal traps into the air, and the last speck of earth is shifted. He is still screaming when from a metre away he spots the submerged body, its head buried in the depths of a ridiculous vertical passageway. He goes on screaming as he drags the rag doll that only yesterday was his brother and is now a piece of mud-battered flesh, and he screams as he pulls him out of his lair. And when at last he sets him down and washes him, slapping water on him as if he were a dirty shoe, he is still screaming.

Big removes the hard pustules from his eyes, his ears and his mouth. Resting his ear against Small's chest, he listens for a heartbeat, but hears nothing. He's not sure if he is dead or alive. He puts his mouth against Small's mouth and blows, and then he presses into his ribs with his hands, and then blows again. He doesn't even know what he is doing, but his movements are driven by instinct and he goes along with it, repeating them as many times as necessary. Nothing happens, there are no changes. His brother doesn't move. The blowing turns into a reverberating cry that travels across their mouths and the compressions turn into violent, unbridled thumps, like blows from a mallet coming down on a casket of bones. He takes him by the shoulders and shakes him against the ground, and he can't stop because his hands are locked into fists and they will not open.

With his head back, his neck twisted and half his face lying in the dirt, at last Small coughs. A long, muddy piece of phlegm is projected from his throat right up to his lips, and he coughs again. Big stops the screaming, the hitting and the blowing and he watches him, motionless, holding his breath.

'Can you hear me?'

There's no answer. And yet Small's chest is moving. A warm breath pushes open his mouth to the day. His fingers clench and unclench with the frailty of a premature child.

'Can you hear me?'

Small coughs again. And before he loses consciousness, as if remembering an ancient grammar, he whispers:

'Forty-three. Forty-one. Seventy-one. Twenty-three. Thirteen. Twenty-nine. Eleven. Eighty-three. Two. Sixty-seven.'

Sitting up, his back against the wall, drinking water. Small spends the afternoon like this, with his torso and legs still covered in earth. Next to him, his brother looks at him with resignation. Neither of them has said another word to the other, until now.

'What have you done?' asks Big.

'Made a hole.'

'I understand that. What I'm asking is why.'

'Because I can't go on in the well. I'm going mad.'

'And you think a hole can help you get out?'

'If I can't get out from up there, I'll get out from below. Even if I have to cross the world like a worm,' says Small defiantly.

Hearing this, Big accepts that the time has come. He can't put it off any longer.

'Get ready. In six days I'm going to get you out of here,' he says, lying down to sleep.

89

OVER THE FINAL five days the routines of the well changed. Big exercised more vigorously than ever, always giving his muscles the necessary rest time for him to fulfil his objective. The food was divided in three and distributed in the following way: half of everything they collected was for the survival kitty which they stored in a makeshift bundle made out of a strip of shirt tied up in tight knots; of the other half, two parts went to Big and the rest was for Small.

Big also helped his brother to recover a certain degree of mental stability. He spent hour upon hour working on memory and coordination; he gave him advice on how to walk further while exerting less energy; he reminded him what he could and couldn't eat and at what times; he told him how to build a den out of branches, and the most suitable places to rest. Above all, he stressed which direction he must take to get home, even though, without the exact coordinates of the well, he himself couldn't be quite sure. He did, at least, have a rough idea of the location of the forest that surrounded them, and he judged that this information would be enough.

Enlivened by the turn of events, Small, for his part, showed a great ability to resist the bouts of delirium that he'd suffered over the previous days. He rigorously memorized every one of his brother's instructions, asking questions whenever he had doubts, or drawing maps in the earth with dry roots. It's true that at night he fell into confused trances that threw him off balance and made him forget who or where he was, but for the best part of the day he remained in his right mind.

They eat in silence a little after sunrise. Big does his warm-up exercises and asks his brother to stretch out his muscles, a request that his brother fulfils without a word, despite his feeble physical state. When they are done, they sit around the survival pack.

'It's time,' says Big. 'You're leaving.'

'Yes.'

'You remember everything I've told you, right?'

'Everything.'

'How do you feel?'

'Nervous. I'm not sure I can do it without you.'

'Sure you can. You're strong like me, or stronger.'

Small's face breaks into a shy smile that does little to hide his immense sadness.

'How do you feel?' he asks.

'Really good. I'm happy you can get out of this hole.'

'I'm happy to get out, too. But I'm not happy to leave you here.'

'Don't worry about that. I'll be fine. In a couple of days you'll come back to find me and we'll go back home together.'

'You promise?'

'Of course I do! Do you promise?'

'What would I do without you?' replies Small, who chokes back a few tears and hugs his brother.

'It's all right now, it's all right now. Let's talk seriously.'

They go over the moves they are going to perform in detail. Big tells his brother the position he must put his body in for the first few seconds, how he has to change his stance after that, and the way to fall so as not to hurt himself. Small jokes about the idea of falling when the ground is, ironically, above him, and this relieves the tension as the moment approaches. The explanations go on. By mid-morning everything has been said, and the sun blesses them with just the right degrees of heat and light. There is nothing left but to do it.

Big is overwhelmed. He knows he will only get one chance and that on that chance both their lives depend. An ice-cold scorpion scuttles up his back. If he fails, if he messes up any of the moves he has so meticulously rehearsed, his brother will die. All these days and weeks making himself strong while his brother has wasted away like a corpse, to the point of weighing so little that a breath of wind could lift him. The methodical repetition of positions and turns, the will to resist… all of it is justified in this one, unrepeatable moment of affirmation and daring.

He can sense the state in which his body will be left after so much strain. It forewarns of his ruin. The strength he is about to use will wrench his bones from their cartilage, break them into pieces, rip apart his muscles like strings from a rope and burst his veins, producing livid, violet haemorrhages under his skin. After the coming effort he will be left twisted like an old doll, and will undoubtedly be unable to move. He is going to burst inside. And he'll be alone. Under these conditions, to survive one day would be a miracle. If his predictions are right and his brother manages to escape from the forest, and if he finds the path to the house and honours his pledge by coming back finally to find him, several days will have passed. At best, his life will no longer depend on him. For the first time.

'Up you get,' he says.
    'Already?'
    'Yes. We can't delay it any longer.'
    'OK. Shall we say goodbye?'
The brothers come together in a long, unrestrained embrace. Big ties the little bindle to a belt loop on Small's

trousers. Afterwards, he scrapes around in a corner and pulls out Mother's old bag of food, which his brother looks at with a sidelong glance, recalling a forgotten nightmare. He tosses it out of the well, and as it hits the ground, cloying fumes of putrid cheese splutter through the seams and it spits out black breadcrumbs and thin, wrinkled figs, decomposed like them.

'Give me your hands,' he says.

Small gives them to him, and as he does he remembers the first day they spent in the well. He goes back to that time, but they are no longer the same; the well is no longer the same. Not even the distance separating them from the world is the same. They take their positions: Big spreading his legs to steady himself when the speed picks up, Small with one knee on the ground so that he isn't dragged along, both of them gripping with such force that their knuckles blanch. And without another thought they start to spin. Big pulls his brother upwards so the rotation is clean and goes on spinning, and Small is raised a hand from the ground and he spins, another hand and he spins, until with the next spin he's virtually horizontal, with his eyes closed and his clenched teeth making dents in his gums; and still they spin, faster and faster, with each spin mapping a bigger circumference, and when it seems like they are at the point of falling, exhausted and breathless from so much spinning, Small slips down to the ground, but doesn't touch it, then soars back up at an angle, and they repeat this twice more, and in the final ascent Big shouts Now and lets go, and with his eyes still closed Small breaks free and he takes off from the earth towards the sun like a comet of bones, and he extends his weightless body, made from a stalk or an arrow, and casts a fine shadow over his brother's face as he flies above the roots into the daylight, and he tumbles several more times before settling like a leaf on the smooth grass that grows just beyond the well.

Laid out on top of it, Small beams. With his hands he caresses the daisy petals, the small stones, the blanket that covers the earth. Everything has changed. The light is different. The smells are different. What a smell, the forest. Thirstily he breathes in the distant perfume of fruit and almonds. He turns his body to rub it against the new colours, to breathe as if for the first time. It feels like he has been born. He cries.

Afterwards he drags himself towards the mouth of the well—mainly because he doesn't want to break the spell that he is caught up in, and secondly to avoid stumbling and being pitched back in again. He pokes his head over and sees his brother sitting in a strange pose with his arms bent backwards and his legs spread out as if they belonged to another body.

'We did it!' Small cries, delightedly.

'Ha ha! I knew it! We're the greatest! Have you hurt yourself?'

'A bit. But I'm fine. Are you OK?'

'Yes, I'm fine.'

They look at each other for a few seconds not knowing what else to say. It feels strange to be so far apart, even if in reality the distance separating them is just a few metres. It's Small who speaks first:

'I think I have to go.'

'Yes.'

'I'll come back for you.'

'Yes. But before that you must keep your promise,' says Big.

'I know.'

'I hope you can.'

'I've thought about it a lot. I won't be afraid.'

Small gets to his feet and collects Mother's bag, which landed a few metres from the well. Then he goes back to the edge to look at his brother for the last time.

'Kill her for what she did to us,' Big says.

And also:

'Remember that she threw us in here. You don't love her anymore.'

*

With those words still sounding through the forest, on the mountains and along every path, Small departs. And huddled in a corner of the well, alone now, Big surrenders himself to a torture that will go on for hours and days, and he utters one last message, which nobody hears, in that capricious language of tears and laughter:

'Amam cor...'

97

SMALL ARRIVES DRENCHED in the orange light of the afternoon. He lets the things he brought with him drop to the ground: a rucksack, two ropes, a small stick, several stakes and a hunting knife. It wasn't hard to find the way back: an invisible cord pulled him from his navel.

Seeing it now, with new eyes, it is a beautiful place to die.

He remains painfully thin. His eyes are still sunken deep in their sockets, as if they were tired of looking. His cheekbones could cut right through the flesh that covers them. He has, however, recovered the olive colour in his face and managed to separate the animal from the man.

He walks slowly towards the well, giving each step its due importance, gauging the distance that separates him from the mouth and which grows shorter with each new step. He stops two metres from the well. He still can't see. Nor does he say anything. Another step. The bottom of the well glistens in the corner of his eye.

The next step is the last. With his hands holding on to the edge, he leans over.

*

The previous days were very strange for him. Not because of the trouble he had finding the way home, or the nights he spent out in the open, imagining himself lost. Not because he went back to eating ripe fruit, but because he bore his brother's absence like a necessary void. He felt as if a shark had ripped his body at the waist, and as he walked along like that—so incomplete, his organs hanging out for all to see, powerless to hide the emptiness and with no way of preserving his dignity—he felt ashamed.

The previous days were very strange for him, with that shame seeping out of every pore on his skin, leaving him slippery for any human contact. Along the dirt paths, in the copper mines, in factories destroyed by desperation, in the cities left to ruin, people made way for him. None of them could stand the glare of his eyes since in them it was still possible to see the well. And yet the people assumed his shame—the obscenity of so many years spent in a daze—and in silence they began to escort him—an unassailable throng, a mob of men and women emerging from their cages.

The previous days were very strange for him, visiting Mother, who seemed to have expected the parting and neither screamed nor put up resistance. He didn't want to know her reasons for doing what she did, but seeing her happy and without remorse was enough for him to understand that there were stories he didn't know. He suffocated her with the old food bag she had left them with in the well—that bait that never broke their spirit—so that she understood, before she went, that they didn't touch a morsel of that false charity, that they overcame every urge, that they did not surrender.

The previous days were very strange for him; the family home surrounded by an expectant crowd, and him, inside, alone, avoiding their gaze. And ultimately leaving, because that place could no longer be his and because he knew that his spirit was no longer close to what it had been before.

'I'm back,' he says.

He unravels the ropes and secures the ends to the stakes nailed into the ground. He takes the opposite end of one of them and ties it around his body, winding three circles around his waist and two more around his groin. An endless human tide observes the ceremony in complete silence, spilling out from the edges of the forest. He tosses the other end of the second rope into the well. Afterwards, he sits down on the edge. And while the night closes its gates above him, announcing the end of an era of darkness, blooming like a cluster of promises in his chest which, despite his death, will keep on growing, he wonders if he should cut the ropes and let himself fall, or if it would be better, after all, to retrieve the rotting corpse of his brother and hold him up as a symbol of insurrection, and for his anniversary to light the darkness with a tremor of footsteps and noise, and for us to wake up tomorrow from this grim dream with the courage of a rising sea, tearing down the walls that silenced us, regaining our ground, having our say.

ACKNOWLEDGEMENTS

This book, like the last one, is the product of much effort and affection. Given that I don't know if I will ever have this opportunity again, I would like to thank all the people who, in one way or another, accompanied me in the process.

To my parents, Rafael and Nieves, for teaching me both to keep my feet on the ground and to lift myself up several hand spans above it; to my sister Adriana for her unstinting faith in me; to the old friends who followed the writing from close by or afar and who helped me: Izas, Jaime, Adriana, Pere, Ángela, Santi, Jesús, Galder, Igor, Ada, Ángel, Pablo and the Parretis Rafa and Mario; to Pedro de Hipérbole, my first passionate reader; to those who spread the word; to the Cantabrian and Mediterranean family.

I owe a special mention to the people of Libros del Silencio, above all my editor, Gonzalo, who believed in me, understood how to guide me, and allowed me to live out a dream. And not forgetting Irene (retrospectively), Marc and Pablo, who worked so hard over many weeks and treated me with respect and friendship. What immense talent you have, all of you.

Thank you to Koldo Asua for lighting the way.

And my thanks to Ana Cristina, for countless reasons: from Quinta da Regaleira to today, now, as someone is reading this page.

PUSHKIN PRESS

Pushkin Press was founded in 1997, and publishes novels, essays, memoirs, children's books—everything from timeless classics to the urgent and contemporary.

Our books represent exciting, high-quality writing from around the world: we publish some of the twentieth century's most widely acclaimed, brilliant authors such as Stefan Zweig, Marcel Aymé, Teffi, Antal Szerb, Gaito Gazdanov and Yasushi Inoue, as well as compelling and award-winning contemporary writers, including Andrés Neuman, Edith Pearlman, Eka Kurniawan and Ayelet Gundar-Goshen.

Pushkin Press publishes the world's best stories, to be read and read again. Here are just some of the titles from our long and varied list. To discover more, visit www.pushkinpress.com.

———

THE SPECTRE OF ALEXANDER WOLF
GAITO GAZDANOV

'A mesmerising work of literature' Antony Beevor

SUMMER BEFORE THE DARK
VOLKER WEIDERMANN

'For such a slim book to convey with such poignancy the extinction of a generation of "Great Europeans" is a triumph' *Sunday Telegraph*

MESSAGES FROM A LOST WORLD
STEFAN ZWEIG

'At a time of monetary crisis and political disorder... Zweig's celebration of the brotherhood of peoples reminds us that there is another way' *The Nation*

BINOCULAR VISION
EDITH PEARLMAN

'A genius of the short story' Mark Lawson, *Guardian*

IN THE BEGINNING WAS THE SEA
TOMÁS GONZÁLEZ

'Smoothly intriguing narrative, with its touches of sinister, Patricia Highsmith-like menace' *Irish Times*

BEWARE OF PITY
STEFAN ZWEIG

'Zweig's fictional masterpiece' *Guardian*

THE ENCOUNTER
PETRU POPESCU

'A book that suggests new ways of looking at the world and our place within it' *Sunday Telegraph*

WAKE UP, SIR!
JONATHAN AMES

'The novel is extremely funny but it is also sad and poignant, and almost incredibly clever' *Guardian*

THE WORLD OF YESTERDAY
STEFAN ZWEIG

'*The World of Yesterday* is one of the greatest memoirs of the twentieth century, as perfect in its evocation of the world Zweig loved, as it is in its portrayal of how that world was destroyed' David Hare

WAKING LIONS
AYELET GUNDAR-GOSHEN

'A literary thriller that is used as a vehicle to explore big moral issues. I loved everything about it' *Daily Mail*

BONITA AVENUE
PETER BUWALDA

'One wild ride: a swirling helix of a family saga... a new writer as toe-curling as early Roth, as roomy as Franzen and as caustic as Houellebecq' *Sunday Telegraph*

JOURNEY BY MOONLIGHT
ANTAL SZERB

'Just divine... makes you imagine the author has had private access to your own soul' Nicholas Lezard, *Guardian*

BEFORE THE FEAST

SAŠA STANIŠIĆ

'Exceptional… cleverly done, and so mesmerising from
the off… thought-provoking and energetic' *Big Issue*

A SIMPLE STORY

LEILA GUERRIERO

'An epic of noble proportions… [Guerriero] is a mistress
of the telling phrase or the revealing detail' *Spectator*

FORTUNES OF FRANCE

ROBERT MERLE

1 *The Brethren*
2 *City of Wisdom and Blood*
3 *Heretic Dawn*

'Swashbuckling historical fiction' *Guardian*

TRAVELLER OF THE CENTURY

ANDRÉS NEUMAN

'A beautiful, accomplished novel: as ambitious as it is generous,
as moving as it is smart' Juan Gabriel Vásquez, *Guardian*

ONE NIGHT, MARKOVITCH

AYELET GUNDAR-GOSHEN

'Wry, ironically tinged and poignant… this is a fable
for the twenty-first century' *Sunday Telegraph*

KARATE CHOP & MINNA NEEDS REHEARSAL SPACE

DORTHE NORS

'Unique in form and effect… Nors has found a novel
way of getting into the human heart' *Guardian*

**RED LOVE: THE STORY OF AN EAST GERMAN
FAMILY**

MAXIM LEO

'Beautiful and supremely touching… an unbearably poignant
description of a world that no longer exists' *Sunday Telegraph*

SONG FOR AN APPROACHING STORM

PETER FRÖBERG IDLING

'Beautifully evocative… a must-read novel' *Daily Mail*